The Atacama Desert

By Lynn Peppas

🌳 Crabtree Publishing Company

www.crabtreebooks.com

Crabtree Publishing Company

www.crabtreebooks.com

Author: Lynn Peppas
Publishing plan research and development:
 Sean Charlebois, Reagan Miller
 Crabtree Publishing Company
Editor and indexer: Wendy Scavuzzo
Design: Margaret Amy Salter
Photo research: Margaret Amy Salter,
 Crystal Sikkens
Project coordinator: Kathy Middleton
**Production coordinator and prepress
 technician**: Margaret Amy Salter
Print coordinator: Katherine Berti

Picture credits:
Alamy: © Prisma Bildagentur AG: page 17
Corbis: © ARIEL MARINKOVIC/epa: page 25
Dreamstime: page 14 (background)
Shutterstock: cover, pages 1, 4, 9, 10, 11 (bottom), 13
 (except viscacha), 16 (left), 19 (top), 24, 27, 28 (bottom)
Thinkstock: pages 5, 6, 8, 12 (bottom), 13 (viscacha),
 20 (background), 28 (top)
Wikimedia Commons: Yerson_O: page 11 (top); Pablo
 Trincado: pages 12 (top), 14 (inset); Hans Peter Möller:
 page 12 (middle); Emilio: page 15; Pedro Subercaseaux
 Errázuriz: page 16 (right); Robin Fernandes: page 18;
 ESO/Yuri Beletsky: page 19 (bottom); Pierre cb: page 20
 (inset); Luca Galuzzi: page 21; Reinhard Jahn, Mannheim:
 page 22; Gobierno de Chile: page 23 (top); Aeveraal: page
 23 (bottom); Carlos yo: page 26

Library and Archives Canada Cataloguing in Publication

Peppas, Lynn
 The Atacama Desert / Lynn Peppas.

(Deserts around the world)
Includes index.
Issued also in electronic formats.
ISBN 978-0-7787-0709-7 (bound).--ISBN 978-0-7787-0717-2 (pbk.)

 1. Atacama Desert (Chile)--Juvenile literature. I. Title.
II. Series: Deserts around the world (St. Catharines, Ont.)

F3131.P46 2012   j983'.14   C2012-905682-0

Library of Congress Cataloging-in-Publication Data

CIP available at Library of Congress

Crabtree Publishing Company

www.crabtreebooks.com   1-800-387-7650

Printed in Canada/102012/MA20120817

Published in Canada
Crabtree Publishing
616 Welland Ave.
St. Catharines, Ontario
L2M 5V6

Published in the United States
Crabtree Publishing
PMB 59051
350 Fifth Avenue, 59th Floor
New York, New York 10118

Published in the United Kingdom
Crabtree Publishing
Maritime House
Basin Road North, Hove
BN41 1WR

Published in Australia
Crabtree Publishing
3 Charles Street
Coburg North
VIC 3058

CONTENTS

Chapter 1: The Atacama Desert 4

Chapter 2: The Atacama's Unique Geography . . . 8

Chapter 3: Living in the Atacama Desert 14

Chapter 4: Travel and Commerce 20

Chapter 5: Desert at Risk 24

Comparing the World's Deserts 28

Timeline 29

Glossary 30

Find Out More 31

Index 32

Words that are defined in the glossary are in
bold type the first time they appear in the text.

CHAPTER 1
The Atacama Desert

The Atacama Desert is one of the driest deserts in the world. It is a hyper-arid desert. It receives 0.04 inches (1 mm) of rain a year. There are some areas of the Atacama Desert that have not received rainfall for over 400 years, or since people began keeping records about the weather.

Parts of the Atacama Desert have been described as looking much like the landscape on the Moon or other planets such as Mars.

Shallow salt lakes such as Laguna Colorada (Red Lake) are found throughout the Atacama Desert.

FAST FACT

A desert is a large, dry area of land that receives very little rainfall. About one-fifth of Earth's surface is desert.

Chile

The Atacama Desert makes up about one-third of the South American country of Chile. Chile's long, thin shape makes it easy to recognize. It is the longest country running in a north-south direction and is 2,672 miles (4,300 km) long. At its widest point, it is only 149 miles (240 km) and for the most part is only about 110 miles (177 km) wide. Argentina and Bolivia border Chile to the east, and Peru borders it to the north. The Atacama Desert is found in the northern part of Chile. The desert is located between the Pacific Ocean on its western side, and the Andes Mountains—the highest mountains in North, Central, or South America—which run along its eastern border. The desert covers an area of about 40,600 square miles (105,154 sq km). It runs about 600 miles (966 km) along the coast of Chile.

5

Hand of the Desert

One dramatic scene that reaches out to passersby in the Atacama Desert is that of *Mano del Desierto* which translated from Spanish to English means "Hand of the Desert." This sculpture of a giant hand emerging from the sands of the Atacama Desert is the work of Chilean artist, Mario Irarrázabal. It is found off the Pan-American Highway about 47 miles (75 km) south of Antofagasta. The sculpture stands 36 feet (11 m) tall and is made of iron and cement. The Hand reaching up from the vast desert sands of the Atacama Desert was designed to make viewers think of loneliness, torture, sorrow, vulnerability, and helplessness.

The giant sculpture called *Mano del Desierto*, or "Hand of the Desert," is a popular tourist attraction in the Atacama Desert.

The Elqui Valley forms the southern border of the Atacama Desert.

NOTABLE QUOTE

*"This **elongated** country is like an island, separated on the north from the rest of the continent by the Atacama Desert — the driest desert in the world, its inhabitants like to say, although that must not be true, because in springtime parts of the **lunar** rubble tend to be covered with a mantle of flowers, like a wondrous painting by Monet."*

—Chilean novelist Isabel Allende describes the Atacama Desert in her published memoir *My Invented Country.*

7

CHAPTER 2

The Atacama's Unique Geography

Chile is divided into three distinct regions of varying landforms and climates. They are northern, central, and southern Chile. The Atacama Desert lies in the northern region of Chile. This region is sometimes split into two smaller regions called El Norte Grande, which means the Grand, Far, or Great North, and El Norte Chico, which means Small or Near North.

The Valle de la Luna, or Valley of the Moon, is considered to be one of the driest places on Earth. Some areas have not received rain for hundreds of years. Its large craters, miles of **desolate** sand and rocky surfaces, strangely carved rocks, and volcanic peaks make it similar to the Moon's surface.

Landforms in the Atacama Desert

The Atacama is a coastal desert. The Pacific Ocean forms its western border. There is no coastal plain and the land rises dramatically in a coastal mountain range known as the Cordillera de la Costa. The mountains in this range have a height of about 4,921–6,562 feet (1,500–2,000 m). Many of these mountains form cliffs into the Pacific Ocean.

Further east, past this mountain range, the land rises into small hills and a flat, high plain or plateau called an **altiplano**. The altiplano is about 11,483–14,764 feet (3,500–4,500 m) above sea level. The altiplano is made up of sand, eroded gravel, and volcanic matter from the Andes Mountains.

The desert's eastern border is the Cordillera Domeyko mountain range which runs parallel to, and is part of, the Andes Mountains. Mountains in this range reach heights of 16,000 feet (4,900 m). These **fold mountains** were created by the upward folding of Earth's crust from the collision of the two **tectonic plates** called the Pacific and South American plates.

FAST FACT

The Cordillera Domeyko mountain range was named after the geologist Ignacy Domeyko. Domeyko was born in Russia but lived most of his life in Chile. He was a well-respected teacher who studied Chile's geography.

9

Volcanoes in the Atacama Desert

The Pacific coast of Chile is home to many volcanoes. A number of these volcanoes lie in the Atacama Desert such as the Licancabur, Ojos del Salado, and the Lascar. Ojos del Salado is the highest volcano above sea level in the world and the second highest peak in the Andes. It stands about 22,615 feet (6,893 m) at its highest point. Its last known eruption took place about 1,000–1,500 years ago. The volcano's Spanish name *Ojos del Salado* means "eyes of salt," which refers to the two huge salt lagoons in the volcano's glacier.

FAST FACT

Climatologists refer to the center of the Atacama Desert as "absolute desert," which is Earth's driest place. Some places at the center of the Atacama have no recorded rainfall. Because there is no moisture, nothing rots. Living things that have died in the absolute desert are almost perfectly preserved.

Salt Lakes

A salt lake is a body of water that does not drain into a river or other body of water. It has a high concentration of salts and minerals. When the water evaporates, it leaves large, dry deposits of salt called a salt flat or salt lake. Salar de Atacama is the largest salt flat in Chile. It covers about 1,158 square miles (3,000 sq km). It is one of the world's largest sources of lithium—a metal used in the production of lithium batteries.

Coastal Desert Climate

The Atacama Desert is a cool, coastal desert. Coastal deserts have cool winters and warm summers. In spring to summer (October to March), the temperatures range from 68–75˚F (20–24˚C) during the day to 32–41˚F (0–5˚C) at night. In fall to winter (April to September), the temperatures range from 59–68˚F (15–20˚C) during the day to 14–32˚F (–10–0˚C) at night.

Chile's longest river—the Loa River—runs through the Atacama Desert. In the 1800s, it supplied much of the water to agricultural towns. In 1911, a pipeline was built that redirected much of the water to mining areas, leaving desert towns with no water for crops or livestock.

El Tatio Geysers

A **geyser** is hot water trapped underground that occasionally discharges hot water or steam into the air. The Andes mountain range is home to many active volcanoes. The Atacama Desert contains over 100 geysers that are located in an area named El Tatio. At El Tatio, water is heated by underground **magma** from the nearby volcanoes, which causes the geysers to erupt. Many of these geysers erupt steam into the air daily just before sunrise. They are located in the northeastern part of El Norte Grande, on the high altiplano, at about 14,108 feet (4,300 m) above sea level. The area is so high that many travelers experience **altitude sickness** with symptoms such as headaches and upset stomach.

The tamarugo tree is native to the Atacama Desert. It is a flowering tree that needs very little water. Its fruit and leaves (shown above and below) are eaten by goats and cattle. It often gets enough water from morning dew in the desert. It can grow in **saline** soils such as those found in the Atacama Desert. These trees grow up to 26–66 feet (8–20 m) tall and are about 32 inches (80 cm) in diameter.

Cactus

Lichen

Flora and Fauna in the Atacama

The Atacama Desert is one of the driest places on Earth. There are some areas of the desert that sustain no life whatsoever. This hyper-arid desert has very little soil or sand. Plants and animals that do live in some areas of the desert have had to adapt to survive. Many live near the coast where dew and fog supply small amounts of water.

Cacti

Cacti such as the tall copao cactus grow in areas close to the coast. These cacti grow to be about 10 feet (3 m) tall and occasionally bear white flowers. The atacameno is a cactus that is short and round, and grows in clumps. It bears yellow flowers at the top in the center of the plant. The stems are a gray color with spines. This cactus has a taproot that is much longer than the stem and stores water for the plant.

Lichens

Lichens are living organisms that consist of at least two essential parts living together: algae and fungus. Lichens have no root systems. They grow in extreme environments such as hyper-arid deserts on locations such as rocks. They have tiny pores that absorb water from fog and dew. Usnea is a type of lichen that grows near the coastal areas of the Atacama Desert.

Animal Adaptations

The Atacama Desert is a harsh environment. Animals living in this desert have had to adapt to the hyper-arid climate. Some animals live in the coastal areas, where the dew and fog provide small amounts of water, whereas others live near the outskirts of the desert in the mountain areas.

Pink Flamingos

Pink flamingos are a favorite tourist attraction at the Los Flamencos National Reserve in San Pedro de Atacama in northern Chile. More than 100,000 tourists visit this nature reserve every year. The reserve is home to many types of birds, including three species of flamingos—the Andean Flamingo, Chilean Flamingo, and James Flamingo.

Taruca

The Taruca is a small species of deer that lives in the mountainous outskirts of the Atacama Desert. As adults, they stand about 2.6–3 feet (70-80 cm) tall and weigh 99–143 pounds (45–65 kg). These animals have sturdy legs that are made for mountain climbing. They are considered an endangered species due to overhunting and habitat loss.

Vicuña

The vicuña is a member of the camel family. It has a long thin neck, small head, and light-brown fur with white underneath. Their mouths are very tough which allows them to eat thorny desert plants. They live in the high altitudes of the plains and mountain areas.

Viscachas are small rodents that live in coastal, rocky areas of the southern Atacama desert. These desert rodents look a lot like rabbits. Adult viscachas often weigh about 6–7 pounds (3 kg) and are often hunted for their meat and fur.

Pink flamingo

Vicuña

Taruca

CHAPTER 3
Living in the Atacama Desert

More than one million people live in Chile's Atacama Desert area. Most people live in large coastal cities, or smaller mining towns, fishing villages, and oasis towns. Antofagasta is the largest city in the Atacama Desert and the third largest city in Chile. It is a coastal port that is sometimes called the "Pearl of the North," because of its economic and historical importance. Antofagasta has a population of more than 300,000 people. It has 12 miles (20 km) of beachfront lands. It is also the center of the world's copper industry.

Chinchorro
One of the first peoples to live in the Atacama Desert were the Chinchorro who settled in the area around 6000 B.C.E. The Chinchorros were one of the first cultures to preserve their dead relatives as mummies. Dry desert conditions are perfect for preserving dead things because there is little moisture to cause rotting.

Atacameño Peoples

The Atacameño peoples arrived in Chile around 9000 B.C.E. and lived at the base of the Andes Mountains in the Atacama Desert. These once **nomadic** peoples learned to farm and raised llamas. They grew crops such as corn, beans, quinoa, and squash. They built canals to carry water for irrigation, aqueducts, and holding ponds.

They traded livestock, crops, textiles, ceramics, baskets, and metals with other villages nearby. The Atacameño people lived in small villages located on high ground and surrounded by defensive walls. Houses were built of stone. Today there are reportedly more than 21,000 people of Atacameño descent living in Chile.

Ancient Geoglyphs

Geoglyphs are designs created in the ground by the Atacameño peoples, possibly thousands of years ago. The designs range from animal, human, and geometric figures. More than 5,000 geoglyphs have been discovered in the Atacama Desert on hillsides, plains, and valley areas. It is not known exactly why they were created. Some educated guesses include that they were forms of worship to ancient gods, or markers for traveling. The geoglyphs were made with stones or by scraping the surface. Some were made using both methods. Some geoglyphs were also painted.

Fast Fact

A geoglyph called Atacama Giant (below) is the world's largest prehistoric human-like figure. It is located in the Atacama Desert at Cerro Unitas. It is 390 feet (119 m) tall and may have been created as far back as 1,500 years ago.

Inca Invasion

Native South Americans from Peru called the Incas invaded northern Chile in 1461. At the time, the Incas were the largest, most powerful empire of native South Americans. Spanish conquistadors came in contact with the Incas in 1526. European illnesses such as smallpox killed many of the Incas because they had no **immunity** against the disease. The Spanish conquered the Incas by 1550 and settled in areas of Chile such as the Atacama Desert.

San Pedro de Atacama Church

The Church of San Pedro de Atacama served as a parish in 1641, although it is believed that it existed over 50 years before that. New walls and archways were added in 1745. It currently serves as a tourist attraction and has been restored and declared a national monument.

Spanish Takeover

The Spanish explorer, Diego de Almagro was the first European to discover Chile. He came to the area in search of silver and gold. He and his party had great difficulties traveling from the east over the Andes mountain range. Many died during the journey. They traveled to a valley in Copiapó and met with another Spaniard who had been expelled from Peru. It was here that Almagro took possession of Chile for the King of Spain. Today, a city named after the Spanish explorer, exists in the Atacama Desert, north of Copaipó. Spanish—the language introduced by Spanish settlers—is still the official language of Chile today.

Diego de Almagro took possession of Chile around 1535 in the Copiapó valley.

Finding Water

The biggest problem for those living in the Atacama Desert is getting fresh water. Copper mining also requires a lot of water. For many years, people had to buy water that was transported by truck to their areas—an expensive process.

People living on the coast get precipitation in the form of a thick fog called camanchaca. A fog-collection project ran from 1987–2002 near the desert village of Chungungo. Large nets were set up on the coastal mountain slopes at El Tofo. The nets collected fog droplets as camanchaca rolled in from the Pacific Ocean.

The water vapor condensed into droplets that dripped down the nets into troughs below. The droplets added up to an average of 3,963 gallons (15,000 L) of water per day. The water ran from the troughs, through a pipe, to a reservoir in nearby Chungungo to be used for drinking and washing, and for watering small vegetable gardens. The project ended in 2003.

Natural aquifers occur in some places in the Atacama. An aquifer is an underground source of water held near the surface by a rock layer. This water can be extracted from wells or natural springs. The freshwater source trickles down rivers that start in the Andes.

Pipelines run from the Andes to the coast to supply fresh water for copper mines and cities in the Atacama Desert.

Oasis Towns

An oasis is an area in the desert where water rises to ground level. The presence of water allows living things to survive. In the Atacama Desert, water is supplied by rivers flowing down from the Andes Mountains.

San Pedro de Atacama is a popular oasis town in the Atacama Desert. It is sometimes called El Oasis.

Fast Fact

Solar power is just starting to be used in the Atacama Desert. A solar park in Copiapó Valley gathers energy from the Sun to pump water from an underground reservoir. The water is used to irrigate crops of grapes grown in the area.

NOTABLE QUOTE

"Oases, at least here in the Atacama, are not found but built. Over thousands of years the channels were dug and lined with stones, then painstakingly cleaned and feasted over every year, to keep the water racing into the fertile ground."

—Lake Sagaris from *Bone and Dream: Into the World's Driest Desert*

Major Roadways

Major roadways in the Atacama Desert were at one time essential for bringing fresh water to cities, towns, and mining areas. They remain a vital trade and commerce link for transporting minerals that are exported from the area.

The Paso de Jama is a mountain pass highway that was constructed in 2005. It is an important trade and commerce link for transporting goods to Bolivia, Argentina, and Paraguay, and the desert city ports in the Atacama.

The Pan-American highway, or Route 5, is a major highway that connects destinations from North and South America. It runs along the western coast of South America, going through large cities in the Atacama Desert such as Arica, Copiapó, and Antofagasta.

Star-gazing

The Atacama Desert has a high altitude, and skies are clear of cloud cover and light pollution. This makes it the perfect place to observe the night skies. For this reason, almost half of the world's astronomical observatories have been built in the Atacama Desert. A famous observatory called Paranal Observatory near Antofagasta attracts astronomers from around the world. This area is known as having one of the darkest night skies on Earth. It was built in 1998 and is home to the Very Large Telescope (VLT) that can peer into **deep space.**

Astronomers study the Milky Way using a laser from one of the four unit telescopes that are part of the VLT.

19

CHAPTER 4

Travel and Commerce

The Atacama Desert offers many unique and fascinating tourist destinations that are found nowhere else on Earth. The desert draws visitors in with glimpses of the well-preserved ancient past in the form of artifacts and mummies. Apart from the past, it is also home to lunar landscapes and views of the heavens that are simply "out of this world." While the Atacama Desert is one of the three top tourist destinations in Chile, mining has been an important industry throughout Chile's history and one of the leading industries since the 1990s. Fishing and farming have also been profitable industries over the years.

Padre Le Paige Museum

Padre Le Paige Museum is one of the best-known museums in South America. It was founded in San Pedro de Atacama in 1963 by a Belgian Jesuit priest named Gustavo Le Paige. The museum displays about 380,000 archaeological objects including more than 4,000 skulls, 1,500 well-preserved mummies, and other interesting artifacts from ancient **indigenous** desert life.

Sandboarding

Sandboarding is similar to snowboarding but, instead of going down snow-covered hills, boarders maneuver down **sand dunes**. The only downfall in sandboarding is there are no ski lifts to take you to the top again. The Atacama Desert is known as one of the premier places to sandboard. Enthusiasts travel to places there such as Iquique and Copiapó for the sandy sport.

Thermal Baths

The Puritama Hot Springs are located about 19 miles (30 km) north from San Pedro de Atacama. Thermal waters from the Puritama River range from 77–91ºF (25–33ºC). The warm waters are said to have great health benefits.

Fast Fact

The Dakar Rally is an annual off-road endurance race that has been labeled as one of the most dangerous off-road races in the world. Since 2009, part of the racecourse travels through the Atacama Desert.

Lauca National Park

Also called the *Parque Nacional Lauca* in Spanish, the Lauca National Park is a protected biosphere reserve that covers an area of about 533 square miles (1,380 sq km). Flamingos, huemul deer, vicuñas, viscachas, and chinchillas are some of the animals that live in the park. The park is also home to two volcanoes. Parinacota is 20,827 feet (6,348 m) high and Pomerape is 20,610 feet (6,282 m) high. The area is also home to the headwaters of the Lauca River and the Chungará and Cotacotani lakes.

Mining in the Atacama Desert

For hundreds of years, mining has been the leading industry in Chile's Atacama Desert. Today mining accounts for about 60 percent of Chile's exports. From the 1500s to the 1800s, silver was mined by the Spanish from the Atacama Desert. In the 1800s, copper, sodium nitrate, or Chile saltpeter, and borax were also mined from the Atacama Desert.

In the early 1900s, two scientists discovered another way to produce sodium nitrate. This caused a decrease in the mining of sodium nitrate in the 1940s. In the 1950s, copper became one of the leading minerals mined in the Atacama Desert. Iron ore, silver, zinc, gold, and potassium nitrate are also mined from the rich deposits found in the desert area.

Today, copper is the leading mineral produced from the Atacama Desert. In fact, Chile is the world's leading producer of copper. The copper is extracted from open-pit mines. The process involves crushing huge quantities of **ore** to extract the smaller amounts of minerals present. For every one ton of copper, about 99 tons (90 metric tons) of waste material is produced.

The open-pit copper mine at Chuquicamata in the Atacama Desert is the largest in the world. It is 2.7 miles (4.3 km) long, 2 miles (3 km) wide, and 2,953 feet (900 m) deep. It produces over 30 percent of the copper in Chile.

Fast Fact

Sodium nitrate has been mined and used for explosives and fertilizers since the mid-1800s. During World War I, more than 3 million tons (2.7 million metric tons) of sodium nitrate was mined from the Atacama Desert for use in explosives.

Copiapó Mining Accident

Mining is a dangerous occupation. Often cave-ins result in death for workers trapped below. On Thursday, August 5, 2010, a cave-in occurred at the San Jose copper and gold mine in the Atacama Desert, north of Copiapó. But, in this case, all 33 of the trapped miners were rescued. They were trapped about 2,300 feet (700 m) underground for a record-breaking 69 days. During that time, fresh air and supplies were sent down to them via a drilled borehole. They were rescued on October 13, 2010.

The miners were brought to the surface in a capsule that was sent down to where they were trapped.

Fishing Industry

In the 1950s, the fishing industry in the Atacama Desert experienced an economic boom. Many workers who were unemployed because of the decline in sodium nitrate mining became commercial fishermen instead. Port cities such as Iquique had dozens of fisheries where fish such as anchovies, sardines, mackerel, and sea bass were processed and shipped around the world. The fishing industry has slowly declined since the mid-1900s. **El Niño**, which caused the warming of coastal waters, depleted fish stocks along the coast.

Farming in the Atacama Desert

Today, farmers grow crops such as olives, tomatoes (below), and cucumbers. They water the crops with drip-irrigation systems that use narrow tubes to water plants at their roots to avoid wasting water. Some water is pumped from underground desert aquifers.

CHAPTER 5
Desert at Risk

Many factors can cause deserts to become at risk. Desertification is one factor that has put the Atacama Desert in jeopardy. Desertification is a process through which once-fertile land becomes a dry, and often lifeless, desert. Factors such as climate change or human mismanagement of the land can bring about desertification. Mining is another threat to the Atacama Desert. While mining has provided economic growth to Chile, it is also putting the desert, animals, plants, and people at risk.

NOTABLE QUOTE

"...the huge plume of brownish black soot coloring the ground for miles around Chuquicamata, the world's largest open-pit copper mine, near Calama, Chile... [has] left a hole so big some people say you can see it from space. Pollution is everywhere these days, but it really stands out in the desert."

—Field notes from *National Geographic* photographer Joel Sartore

Desertification

Desertification is a global problem that is occurring in many areas on Earth, including the Atacama Desert. Its side effects are devastating to the soil, people, plants, and animals in surrounding areas.

The roots of plant life such as grasses and trees hold the soil in place. When plant life disappears, the soil is easily blown away by the winds or washed away by rain. Areas of grasslands overgrazed by cattle can quickly lose their soil, too. In central Chile, desertification also results from deforestation, or the clearing of large forested areas for agricultural lands. The land becomes a desert and cannot sustain any forms of life.

It is estimated that 62 percent of Chile's land suffers from desertification and that the desert is advancing 1,312 feet (400m) every year. But scientists and people in the community are working toward reversing the process with organizations such as CONAF—the National Forest Corporation—in Chile.

CONAF

CONAF is the Corporacion Nacional Forestal, or the National Forest Corporation. This government agency works toward protecting forests and the environment in areas of Chile such as in and near the Atacama Desert. The organization started a tree-planting program in 2011. Their goal is to plant one tree for every person in Chile, or 17 million trees. They want to have a tree planted in front of every house and a small indoor fruit tree in every house. CONAF encourages people to take responsibility for the well-being of their trees.

Members of CONAF help to put out wildfires that start in Chile's forests. This man is at a wildfire just south of Chile's capital city, Santiago.

Water Crisis

Mining uses large quantities of water for operation. The industry taps into river systems and groundwater resources that are already in high demand in the hyper-arid desert area. Taking water from these resources dries out natural wetlands and threatens species of animals that are already challenged by the dry conditions of the desert. The lack of freshwater resources also threatens communities of people living in the towns and cities in the Atacama Desert. Obtaining water becomes expensive and people are forced to move.

Pollution from Mining

Smelter emissions pollute the air and make living conditions near copper mines dangerous for workers. At the Chuquicamata copper mine, the atmosphere and groundwater had high levels of arsenic contamination. Arsenic is a by-product of processing copper and other minerals. In 2005, the national mining company Codelco relocated an entire town of workers and their families about 12 miles (20 km) away to another town called Calama. People living close to the processing plants were experiencing severe health problems.

Pollution in Rivers

Sewage treatment systems process, or clean, wastewater by removing contaminants. They are expensive to build and, up until the 1990s, contaminated water from mining operations, homes, and agricultural areas was simply dumped into nearby rivers such as the Loa River—the Atacama Desert's longest river. Chile's National Environmental Commission (CONAMA) has worked toward improving the wastewater treatment in areas such as the Atacama Desert.

Copper-mining waste along with household, agricultural, and industrial sewage from Santiago has contaminated the Mapocho River.

Overmining

More people are using alternatives to traditional gasoline-powered cars. Lithium—a metal used for making batteries for electric cars—is becoming more in demand. The metal is also used in the production of rechargeable batteries to power technology such as cell phones and laptop computers. Lithium is found in the Atacama only down to a maximum of 131 feet (40 m) below the surface of salt lakes, or salares. Salar de Atacama is said to contain almost 30 percent of Earth's lithium reserves.

Organization for Economic Co-operation and Development (OECD)

In 2010, Chile became the first South American country to join the international organization called OECD. The OECD has created a set of environmental standards that must be followed. Chile tried to join in the past, but was unable to join due to their environmental practices. Environmental reforms Chile has made, and has planned for the future, have since allowed the country to become a member of the organization.

The Salar de Atacama is also home to flamingos that nest in the area. Lithium mining threatens species that make the salt lakes their home.

COMPARING THE WORLD'S DESERTS

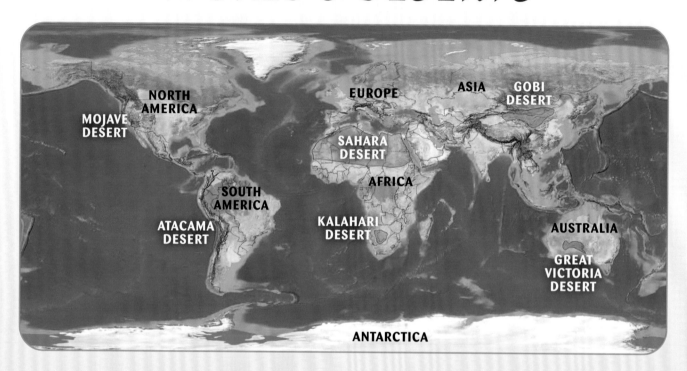

	Continent	Approximate Size	Type of Desert	Annual Precipitation	Natural Resources
Atacama	South America	40,600 square miles (105,154 sq km)	coastal desert	0.04 inches (1 mm)	copper, sodium nitrate, salt, lithium
Gobi	Asia	500,000 square miles (1,294,994 sq km)	cold desert	2–8 inches (5–20 cm)	Oil, coal, copper, gold, petroleum, salt
Great Victoria	Australia	161,700 square miles (418,800 sq km)	hot, dry desert	8–10 inches (20–25 cm)	gold, opal, iron ore, copper, coal, oil
Kalahari	Africa	275,000 square miles (712,247 sq km)	semi-arid desert, arid savannah	5–25 inches (13–64 cm)	coal, copper, nickel, and diamonds
Mojave	North America	25,000 square miles (64,750 sq km)	hot, dry desert	2–6 inches (5–15 cm)	copper, gold, solar power
Sahara	Africa	3.5 million square miles (9.1 million sq km)	hot, dry desert	3 inches (8 cm)	coal, oil, natural gas, various minerals

TIMELINE

About 9000 B.C.E.	Atacameño peoples settle in Atacama Desert area
About 6000 B.C.E.	Chinchorro people settle in Atacama Desert
About 512 C.E.	The geoglyph known as the Atacama Giant is created by the Atacemeño peoples
About 1300	Ojos de Saledo volcano erupts
1461	Incas from Peru invade and move into the Atacama Desert
1535	Spanish conquistador Diego de Almagro is first European to discover Chile's Atacama Desert
1550	Spanish conquer the Incas and settle in Chile, north of Santiago
About 1745	The Church of San Pedro de Atacama is built
February 1879	The War of the Pacific begins between Chile and the combined forces of Bolivia and Peru
October 20, 1883	The Treaty of Ancón concludes the War of the Pacific
1911	A pipeline that diverts water from the Loa River to the copper mining town of Chuquicamata is built
1963	Padre Le Paige Museum is founded
1987	Fog collection begins off Pacific Coast at El Tofo mountain
1992	*Mano del Desierto* (Hand of the Desert) sculpture is unveiled in the Atacama Desert
1994	Chile's Congress creates the National Environmental Commission (CONAMA)
1997	NASA tests rover vehicle Nomad at Valley of the Moon in the Atacama Desert near San Pedro de Atacama.
1999	Paranal Observatory is opened near Antofagasta, Chile
2005	Paso de Jama highway is constructed as a trade and commerce link between Bolivia, Argentina, Paraguay, and the Atacama ports
2009	The Dakar Rally international off-road endurance race is moved to South America and travels through parts of the Atacama Desert
2010	Chile joins the Organization for Economic Co-operation and Development (OECD)
August 5, 2010	Cave-in at the San Jose gold and copper mine traps 33 miners underground. All survive and are rescued 69 days later.

GLOSSARY

altiplano A high, flat plateau or plain

altitude sickness An illness felt by people who are unaccustomed to living in high places

aquifers Naturally occurring underground water beds usually held by a layer of rock or gravel

deep space The area in space that is beyond Earth's solar system

desolate Lacking the presence of living things

El Niño An unusual flow of warm surface waters from the Pacific Ocean current that disrupts the typical climate

elongated Long and stretched out

evoke to call up or depict

fold mountain A mountain that was created by the upward push of two tectonic plates

geoglyphs Large-scale works of art that are created on Earth's surface

geyser A hot spring of water that occasionally jets water or steam into the air

immunity The body's ability to fight a disease or illness

indigenous Growing, living, or occurring naturally in a particular area

lunar Of or relating to the Moon

magma Extremely hot, liquid rock found underneath Earth's surface

nomadic Does not have a fixed home, but instead moves from place to place

Ore Rock that contains minerals such as copper or gold

saline Containing salt

sand dune A ridge or hill of sand that has been piled up by the wind

taproot A thick plant root that grows straight downward

tectonic plate Large layers, or plates, that form Earth's crust

FIND OUT MORE

BOOKS

Allaby, Michael. *Deserts*. Chelsea House, 2006.

Harris, Nathaniel. *Atlas of the World's Deserts*. Fitzroy Dearborn, 2003.

Hyde, Natalie. *Desert Extremes* (Extreme Nature). Crabtree Publishing Company, 2009.

Star, Fleur. *Desert* (Eye Wonder). DK Publishing, 2007.

WEBSITES

The Driest Place on Earth
http://ngm.nationalgeographic.com/ngm/0308/feature3/

Principal Deserts of the World
www.factmonster.com/ipka/A0778851.html

Deserts: Geology and Resources
http://pubs.usgs.gov/gip/deserts/contents/

Desertification
http://pubs.usgs.gov/gip/deserts/desertification

INDEX

altiplano 9, 11
Andes Mountains 5, 9, 10, 11, 15, 16, 17, 18
animals
  adaptations 13
  flamingos 13, 21, 27
  in Lauca National Park 21
  livestock 15, 25
  llamas 15
  taruca 13
  vicuñas 13, 21
  viscachas 13, 21
Antofagasta 14
Atacama Giant 15

climate 11
coastal areas 5, 9, 10, 13, 17
CONAF 25
cordilleras 9

Dakar Rally 21
de Almagro, Diego 16
desert, defined 5
desertification 24, 25
Domeyko, Ignacy 9

El Niño 23
El Tatio geysers 11

farming 15, 23, 25
fishing industry 20, 23

geoglyphs 15
geysers 11

"Hand of the Desert" 6, 29
highways 19
hot springs 21

Incas 16
irrigation 15, 18, 23

land area 5
landscape 4, 8, 9
location 5

Mano del Desierto 6, 29
map 9
mining 14, 17, 22, 24, 26-27
  Chiquicamata pollution 26
  Copiapó accident 23
  copper 14, 17, 26
  lithium 10, 27
  sodium nitrate 22
mountains 5, 9
  Andes 5, 9, 10, 11, 15, 16, 17, 18
  coastal 9, 17
mummies 14, 20

Norte Grande 8, 11

oasis towns 18
observatories 19
OECD 27
Ojos del Salado 10

Padre Le Paige Museum 20
Pan-American highway 18
parks
  Lauca National Park 21
  Los Flamencos National Reserve 13
  solar power 18
Paso de Jama 19
peoples
  Atacameño 15
  Chinchorro 14

plants
  adaptations 12
  cacti 12
  crops 15, 23
  desertification 25
  flowering 7
  lichens 12
  protecting forests 25
  tamarugo tree 12
pollution 24, 26
population 14, 15
Puritama Hot Springs 21

rainfall 4, 8, 10
regions 8
rivers 11, 17, 18, 21, 26
  Loa River 11, 26, 29
roadways 19

Salar de Atacama 10, 27
salt lakes 10, 27
San Pedro de Atacama
  church 16
  oasis town 18
sandboarding 21
Spaniards 16, 22

threats 24-27
tourism 20, 21
trade 15, 19

Valley of the Moon 8
volcanoes 8, 9, 10, 11, 21

water pipelines 11, 17, 26
water sources 11, 15, 18, 23, 26
  aquifers 17, 23
  fog 13, 17